BASS FEVER
Fishing Cartoons

by Bruce Cochran

Copyright © 1991 by Bruce Cochran

Published by
Willow Creek Press
An imprint of NorthWord Press, Inc.
Box 1360 Minocqua, WI 54548

ISBN 1-55971-127-2

Willow Creek Press

Library of Congress Cataloging-in-Publication Data

Cochran, Bruce.
    Bass fever : fishing cartoon / by Bruce Cochran.
        p.   cm.
    ISBN 1-55971-126-4 (hardcover) : $12.50, -- ISBN 1-55971-127-2
(softcover)
    1. Fishing--Caricatures and cartoons.   2. American wit and humor,
Pictorial.   I. Title.
NC 1429.C61A4   1991
741.5'973--dc20

                                                            91-12694
                                                              CIP

For information on other Willow Creek
titles, write or call 1-800-336-5666.

Designed by Mary Shafer
Typography by KR Design
Printed in the USA

For Carol,
my favorite fishing buddy.

About the Author

Cartoonist Bruce Cochran brings his humor to us from a broad background in the outdoors as well as the arts.

Graduating from Oklahoma University with his Bachelor's in Design, he worked for Hallmark Cards as a writer/illustrator, and soon moved on to freelancing jobs with such publications as *Playboy, Look, The Saturday Evening Post, Sports Afield* and *Field & Stream.*

Cochran also has to his credit a daily sports section cartoon feature, "Fun 'N' Games with Cochran!" in the nation's #1 selling newspaper, *USA TODAY.* His children's book, *No Mind for Wellington,* first published in 1972 (Holt, Rinehart & Winston) is still in print today.

His interest in the outdoors makes him an avid hunter, fisherman and a collector of antique duck decoys. A sponsor member of Ducks Unlimited, his watercolors have been exhibited at the Easton, MD Waterfowl Festival and the National Ducks Unlimited Wildlife Art Show, among others.

Cochran is married to his wife of 32 years, has two children and has, he says, "been trained by a succession of three Labrador retrievers."

"Your Dad can hardly wait till spring."

"Your distance is O.K. Now work on your accuracy!"

"Wake up! You were fishing in your sleep again!"

"Whaddaya mean there's nothing to do tonight? I rented 'jig-fishing on municipal water treatment facilities' and make 'make your own buzzbaits from old car bodies!'"

"What are your hobbies?"

"Don't bother to wrap them, I'll eat them here."

"The perfect lure for you: a jerk bait."

"It was owned by a little old lady who only used it for crappie fishing."

"Ah, the first crankbait of spring!"

"Where do you think the bass will be when the water's this cold?"

"The single most important invention in the history of mankind?
It's gotta be the plastic worm!"

"1988. That was a good year for nightcrawler scent."

"Uh…come here a second!"

"Set the hook real hard. It's probably a lunker."

*"I **hate** weekends!"*

"We're using Jimmy Houston sunglasses and Rick Clunn lures! How the hell did we get skunked?!"

WHAT TO DO WHEN THE BASS AREN'T HITTING

"You wouldn't believe the guy I just got away from!
I'll bet he weighed 300 pounds!"

"You know that rock you said I was snagged on? It just jumped."

"You want this lure? Do the laundry and make the beds
for six months and it's yours."

"*Your Dad is furthering his education.
He's going to a seminar on plastic worms.*"

"*Loosen your drag!!*"

"I'll trade you a Reggie Jackson, a George Brett, and a Jose Canseco
for a Rick Clunn."

"I'm not hitting **that!** That's last year's color."

"…don't let him horse you in! Wiggle your tail! That's it! Now jump!…"

"Mrs. Otteson won't let me do a book report on
'Fishing the Crankbait in Heavy Structure.'"

31

"The pH is perfect. The water temperature and barometric pressure are ideal. Wonder why the bass aren't hitting…"

"Hey Marvin! That guy who brought in the
teeny-weeny little bass is here!"

"You could have put him on a smaller board so he'd look bigger."

"These old strip pits are hard to get into.
That's why they're full of bass!"

"First kill one large chicken…"

"It looks great, but what happens when your wife misses this pair of panty hose?"

"Eat your heart out, Dave Whitlock!"

"The bass will think it's a calf that's fallen into the water. Right?"

THE SNAP-YOUR-BUG-OFF CAST

THE SCARE-HELL-OUT-OF-THE-BASS CAST

42

"Remember that bass bug you tied that looks like a mouse?…"

"Poor thing! What happened to your **tail?**"

*"I spent three hours tying this popper
and I'm not losing it in a damn tree!"*

"What do you think? Does the shredded shower curtain give it more fish appeal?"

"So you got a bite. Big deal."

"*Your guide will be a little late. He got lost on the way over.*"

"No sense going out now. Bass never feed this time of day."

"I can't help you with lure selection right now. The computer is down."

"Get him in the boat first. Then you can play with him!"

"With a plastic worm it's sometimes a good idea to let him take it awhile, but in this case I'd go ahead and set the hook if I were you."

"Is this the secret place you were telling us about?"

55

"We release all the bass we catch, kid. Let' em live to fight again. Besides, I don't want to get this $20,000 boat all slimey."

"I'm a small mouth bass. My wife here is a large mouth."

"…room deodorizer…bug repellent…antacids. Yep!
You're ready for Uncle Charlie's."

"I know it's hard to believe, but I made this boat myself."

"If anything ever happens to Uncle Charlie
the duct tape industry will never recover."

"He says he learned it from a bear."

"Don't fish off the dock. I save it for little kids."

"We won't need an alarm clock. When we smell Uncle Charlie's coffee we'll have to get out of bed to throw up."

"Mom's pancakes are fluffier but she doesn't let us drink beer with them."

"A little water in the boat is good, kid. Keeps your feet cool."

"See that downed tree, kid? It was standing upright
'til I tied a big stringer of bass to it."

"Let it sit there 'til the circles disappear...

...twitch it once, then hang onto your hat!"

"Don't spill any of this chili on the floor. The dog will roll in it,
then I'll have to pick the hair out and re-heat it."

"What's the matter? Too much shad scent in the chili for you?"

"He broke twenty pound test line but I dove in
and hauled him out by the gills!…

…his head hung over one side of the boat
and his tail hung over the other…

"…couldn't weigh him at the grocery store. Had to haul him out to the highway and weigh him on the truck scales…

…I'd show him to you but I gave him to the high school football team to use as a blocking sled."

*"Now that I've showed you guys how to play poker
it's time to do a little night fishing."*

"You guys head on up the lake. I'll take the kid to my secret place."

"We're either downwind from the fish-cleaning barrel or Uncle Charlie."

*"**I told** you they could jump, kid! Now we'll have to let him flop
'til he wears himself out, then cut the tree down."*

"Put this on your hook, kid. I found it crawling around in my beard."

"Get the net, kid! And the wrench and the screwdriver!"

"If that tree was a bass you'd have scared
him into giving up by now, kid."

"It's my pattern, kid. I fish the shallows with top-water baits early.
Switch to plastic worms at mid-morning, then sleep till late afternoon."

"★@!★!!@ rod came apart again!
They just don't make duct tape like they used to!"

"See if you can pick this backlash out for me, kid.
My eyes aren't as good as they used to be."

"We got a little problem here, kid. Hand me that duct tape."

"We turned the big ones loose but we saved these little five-pounders for supper."

"Don't cut off the heads and tails, kid. Gives you something to hang onto while you're eatin' em."

"What we don't eat tonight we can have for breakfast if we don't run out of syrup."

"The secret of frying fish is to get your grease good and hot."

"I can't even see into Uncle Charlie's coffee with polarized glasses!"

"Uncle Charlie's always talking about a huge bass he keeps losing,
but you know how he exaggerates."

"Don't spill any of your coffee on my boat. It'll take the paint off."

"You should have seen the bass I caught, Mom!
His head hung over one end of the boat and his tail hung over the other!
Had to weight him on the truck scales…"

"If it won't all fit in a car it damn sure won't fit in a canoe."

"If we can't get it here we don't need it."

82

"Maybe we should have left the cream separator
and the fondue set behind."

"There's not much river left now that the
corps of engineers is through with it."

"I can't wait to tie into one of those scrappy little smallmouths on this ultra-light rod!"

"Is this the rock you wanted us to watch out for?"

"Quick! f 5.6 at 500!"

"*I thought you said watch out for that **log!***"

"*I **told** you it was too windy to fly fish!*"

"Tell him he can have a can of lima beans and some cheese
if he'll give us back our fish."

"If I was a smallmouth I'd hang around those rocks over there."

"Hang on a minute. I want to cast around that rock a few more times."

"I told you we'd see lots of wildlife on this trip."

"Mom says the postman and I can enter the father-son bass tournament."

"Now let me get this straight: You bought $500 worth of new tackle so you could enter a tournament where first prize is a $200 trolling motor?"

"He's testing his new fish locator."

"*I found a sponsor for the bass tournament!*"

"*I hope that was just our tackle boxes that blew out back there. I'd hate to go all day without **food!***"

"This isn't basketball, son. Don't slam-dunk them into the live well."

"I hit a crank bait. What'd you hit?"

…"so I see this big purple worm swimming along. How am I to know it's plastic? So I slam it. Right? Next thing I know I'm in a live well. Guy weighs me, turns me loose. He gets a prize, I don't get diddly."

"You don't really appreciate freedom till you've done time in a live well."

"We missed out on first place but I won an anchor and
Dad was voted Mr. Congeniality."

"How can you have cabin fever? You went fishing three days ago."

"What do you mean, 'the **off** season'? It's time to tie bass bugs, build rods, watch fishing shows on TV, stock up on tackle, and don't forget ice fishing, and…"